Perspectives

Living Together

Which Creature Benefits?

Flying Start
to Literacy®

Contents

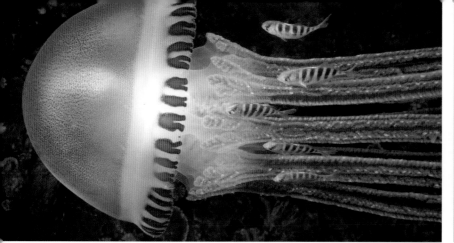

Introduction

Symbiotic relationships: Who wins, who loses?

Sometimes two different kinds of organisms live together and either one or both depend on this relationship for survival. This is called a symbiotic relationship.

Not all symbiotic relationships are beneficial to both partners. In some relationships, both partners benefit; in other relationships, one thrives and the other is unaffected. And sometimes, one animal benefits, while the other is harmed or even dies.

All organisms are part of an ecosystem. Whether the relationship between these living things is a win–win for both, or a loss for one, what would happen if these relationships did not exist? What are the wider benefits for the ecosystem in which they live?

Killer wasps

Read about this wasp. Is it part of a win-win
relationship? asks Joshua Hatch.

What creature – or creatures – benefits?

I'm going to tell you about an animal that might make you grimace. This animal does some pretty nasty things. But keep an open mind because it may be more of a friend to you than you realise.

The animal I'm talking about is a wasp. It's a particular type of wasp, and it isn't actually one animal – it's a whole group of them. They belong to a group of animals that are called parasitoids. They need a host to survive, but they always kill the host.

What makes these wasps special is how they reproduce. They lay eggs, though that part isn't so special. But where they lay their eggs *is* special. They don't use nests or hives. Instead, they lay their eggs on or – in some cases – in other animals. Mostly, they lay their eggs in caterpillars, but they also lay them in beetles, flies and even spiders.

A wasp lays eggs in a tunnel used by solitary bees. When the eggs hatch, the wasp larvae will feed on the bee larvae.

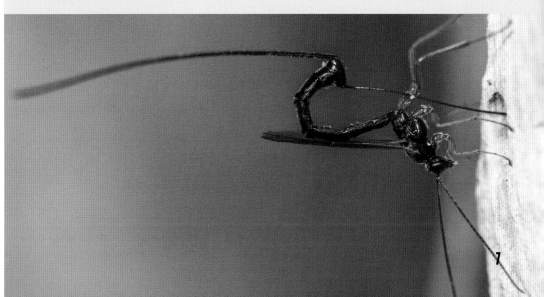

One type of these wasps lands on and then paralyses bugs with its stinger. Then the wasp lays eggs on its paralysed host. Once the eggs hatch, the larvae eat the host animal. That's the end for the bugs!

Another type of this wasp does something even more grisly. They land on other bugs, and instead of paralysing the hosts, the wasps inject their eggs into them.

Then, once the eggs hatch, the larvae eat the host from the inside out as the larvae grow into adults. It's a pretty clever way for parasitoid wasps to give their offspring a safe place to hatch and a built-in food supply. Not so great for the host, though.

This caterpillar has been paralysed by the larvae of a parasitoid wasp.

Parasitoid wasp eggs on a paralysed tomato hornworm, a major pest in gardens

So, why would the parasitoid wasp be a friend to humans? Think about this: every time a wasp lays its eggs, that's the end of the fly or other insect.

That's the reason farmers sometimes raise parasitoid wasps – they are a natural killer of bugs that eat farmers' crops. It might be a win-lose relationship for the wasps and the bugs they use as nurseries, but for farmers and wasps, it's a win-win: the wasps get a place to live and the farmers have a natural way to manage crop-eating pests.

But are the farmers interfering with a natural system by breeding and releasing these wasps?

The
cassowary

This bird is endangered. There are only about 1,500 to 2,000 cassowaries left in the world. Does it matter? asks Kerrie Shanahan. Read about the cassowary to make up your mind.

Gardener of the rainforest

The cassowary is a large bird that cannot fly. It lives in the rainforests in Queensland, Australia, where it roams throughout a large area. It eats various fruits and then spreads the seeds of these plants all over the forest in its droppings. It is an endangered species.

The cassowary needs the forest – the forest is its home. And the forest needs the cassowary. This is a mutualistic relationship.

The cassowary helps disperse the seeds of about 240 rainforest trees and plants. The seeds of at least 70 tree and plant species can be spread only by the cassowary, which can disperse them over long distances. The cassowary can also disperse the seeds of some plants that are toxic to other animals.

So, what effect does this have on the ecosystem? More room for the cassowary?

Without the cassowary, the rainforest will change; it will become less diverse as trees and plants die out. Some people call the cassowary the "gardener of the rainforest"!

A rainforest ecosystem

The cassowary is vital to the health of the rainforest ecosystem. This includes the plants and the animals that live there. That's right, animals need the cassowary, too!

Many rainforest animals eat plants and live in the trees. If cassowary numbers drop, fewer seeds will be dispersed and fewer new plants will grow. Without these plants and trees, what would the animals eat? Where would they live?

The mahogany glider is one animal that lives in the same habitat as the cassowary. It eats nectar, sap and pollen from a type of tree called Myrtaceae trees. What is so special about these trees? The cassowary eats the fruit of these trees, too, and disperses their seeds so that new trees will grow. The mahogany glider needs these new trees as a food source.

Many animals share the rainforest with the cassowary and would be affected if the cassowary disappears. Why do you think the cassowary is called the "gardener of the rainforest?" Will it matter if it vanishes?

These animals depend on rainforest plants.

Paradise kingfisher

Mahogany glider

Spotted-tailed quoll

Magnificent brooding frog

Northern red-throated skink

Parasite
got your tongue?

Look closely at this fish's mouth. Can you see the tiny white louse that lives there?

In this article, biologists Kate Mason and Briony Norton figure out which of these creatures benefits from the relationship. What questions do you have about the fish and the louse?

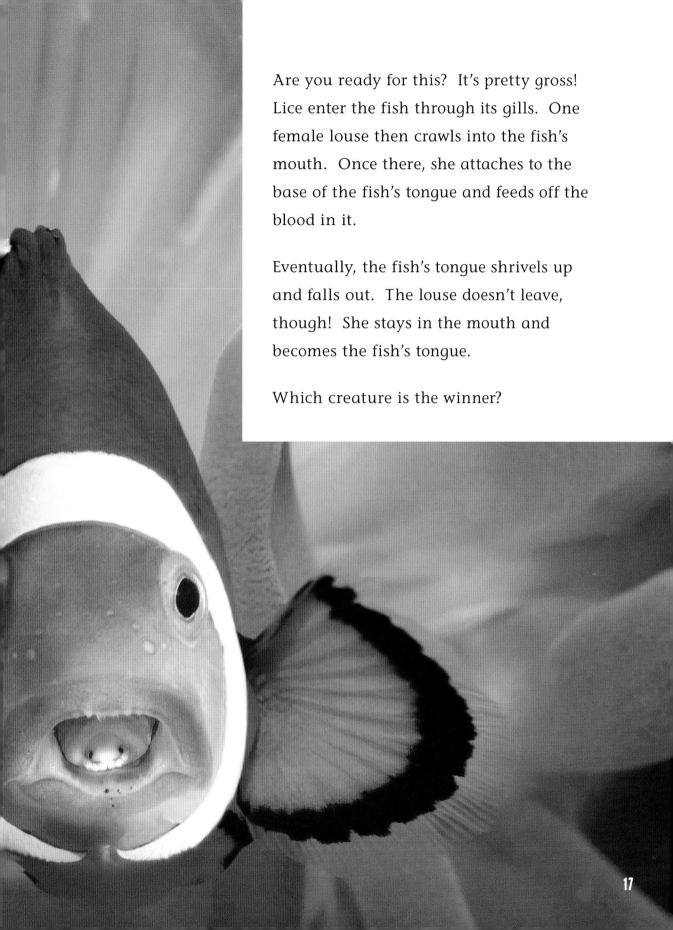

Are you ready for this? It's pretty gross! Lice enter the fish through its gills. One female louse then crawls into the fish's mouth. Once there, she attaches to the base of the fish's tongue and feeds off the blood in it.

Eventually, the fish's tongue shrivels up and falls out. The louse doesn't leave, though! She stays in the mouth and becomes the fish's tongue.

Which creature is the winner?

Here are some questions scientists might ask about the fish and louse.

Is the relationship good for the louse? YES!

Two factors are important for an animal's survival: getting food and reproducing.

The fish provides food for the louse. A female louse attaches to the fish's tongue and sucks blood from it. Blood has healthy nutrients that help the young lice grow into adults. Meanwhile, male lice attach to the gills and feed there.

The fish is also a safe place for the louse to have its young. When the louse has matured in the fish's mouth and replaced its tongue, it mates with the male lice and gives birth to baby lice in the mouth. The first job of the babies is to find a new fish to live in, to start the cycle again.

Is the relationship good for the fish? NO!

When a fish has a louse instead of a tongue, it can't eat properly and can't get the nutrients it needs. As a result, it won't grow properly and will be smaller than normal. The fish also loses a lot of blood because the louse feeds on its blood.

Eventually, these problems can cause the fish to become sick and die. But the louse doesn't cause the fish to die too quickly – it stays alive long enough for the louse to become an adult, mate and give birth to a new generation of lice.

Have the two animals evolved to live together?

These lice have hooked legs that help them attach to the fish's mouth. Their body shape also makes them well suited for living inside a fish's mouth and functioning as a replacement tongue.

As far as we know, the fish doesn't have any special features that suggest it needs or wants the louse to live inside it.

So this is an example of parasitism, which means one animal benefits (louse) while the other is harmed (fish). The louse is the winner!

A dog's life

The partnership between dogs and people is the oldest symbiotic relationship involving animals and humans, writes Kerrie Shanahan.

But are we spending too much money on our furry friends? Why do we pamper them? To make our dogs happy or to make ourselves feel good?

Our best friend

Some experts believe the partnership between dogs and humans started over 30,000 years ago. Dogs helped people hunt, tend herds of goats and sheep, and alert others if danger was coming. In return, they got food, shelter and protection.

Today, this relationship is much more than just two species benefitting from living closely together. For many of us, our dogs are part of the family!

There are almost 5 million dogs in Australia and half a million dogs in New Zealand, and the dog population is increasing faster than the human population. About 38 per cent of Australian households have at least one dog. In New Zealand, about one third of all households has a dog.

Average spending by Australian dog owners per year:

Food (including treats and vitamins) $800

Vet fees $500

Grooming $90

Toys $30

Kennel boarding $200

That's about $1,620 a year

But have we gone too far?

Today, there is no limit to the amount of money some people spend on their dogs. And some dogs have become celebrities. Is it still a win–win relationship with humans?

Top Dog

The most followed dog on social media is a Pomeranian called Jiffpom. He has over 30 million followers across all social media platforms.

Most expensive puppy in the world

A Tibetan mastiff puppy sold for $1.9 million dollars!

Dog hotels

A stay for your pooch at a luxury
dog hotel can cost over $200 a night.
The amenities for your dog may
include a deluxe room, a gym,
a chauffeur, a spa, grooming
services and play areas –
as well as gourmet
dog food!

What is your opinion? How to write a persuasive argument

1. State your opinion

Think about the issues related to your topic. What is your opinion?

2. Research

Research the information you need to support your opinion.

Related *Perspectives* book   Internet   Other sources

3. Make a plan

Introduction

How will you "hook" the reader?

State your opinion.

List reasons to support your opinion.

What persuasive devices will you use?

Reason 1	**Reason 2**	**Reason 3**
Support your reason with evidence and details.	Support your reason with evidence and details.	Support your reason with evidence and details.

Conclusion

Restate your opinion. Leave your reader with a strong message.

4. Publish

Publish your persuasive argument.

Use visuals to reinforce your opinion.